SHANTINIKE'

THE
BOLPUR SCHOOL
OF
RABINDRANATH TAGORE

BY

W. W. PEARSON

ILLUSTRATED BY
MUKUL CHANDRA DEY

New York

THE MACMILLAN COMPANY
1916
All Rights Reserved

TO

JADAV

CONTENTS

SHANTINIKETAN

THE BOLPUR SCHOOL OF
RABINDRANATH TAGORE

The Shantiniketan School Song

BY RABINDRANATH TAGORE

Translated from the original Bengali by the author

*She is our own, the darling of our hearts, the
  Shantiniketan.*
Our dreams are rocked in her arms.
*Her face is a fresh wonder of love everytime we see
  her,*
For she is our own, the darling of our heart.

In the shadows of her trees we meet,
In the freedom of her open sky.
Her mornings come and her evenings
Bringing down heaven's kisses,
*Making us feel anew that she is our own, the
  darling of our heart.*

The stillness of her shades is stirred by the wood-
land whisper;
Her amlaki groves are aquiver with the rapture of
leaves.
She dwells in us and around us however far we
may wander.
She weaves our hearts in a song making us one in
music,
Tuning our strings of love with her own fingers,
And we ever remember that she is our own, the
darling of our heart.

SHANTINIKETAN

INTRODUCTION BY
RABINDRANATH TAGORE

INTRODUCTION

RABINDRANATH TAGORE

The greatest teachers in ancient India, whose names are still remembered, were forest dwellers. By the shady border of some sacred river or Himalayan lake they built their altar of fire, grazed their cattle, harvested wild rice and fruits for their food, lived with their wives and children in the bosom of primeval nature, meditated upon the deepest problems of the soul and made it their object of life to grow in sympathy with all creation and in communion with the Supreme Being. There students flocked round them and had their lessons of immortal life in the atmosphere of truth, peace and freedom of the spirit.

Though in later ages circumstances changed and numerous kingdoms, great and small, flourished in wealth and power, and forests began to give way to towns with multiplication of luxuries in the homes of the rich, the highest ideals of civilization in our country ever remained the ideals, of those forest sanctuaries. All our great classic poets in their epic verses and dramas looked back with reverence upon that golden daybreak of the awakenment of India's soul.

In the modern time my turn has also come to dream of that age towering above all ages of the subsequent history in the greatness of its simplicity and wisdom of pure life. While spending a great part of my youth in the riverside solitude of the sandbanks of the Padma a time came when I woke up to the call of the spirit of my country and felt impelled to dedicate my life in furthering the purpose that lies in the heart of her history. I seemed choked for breath in the hideous nightmare of our present time, meaningless in its petty ambitions of poverty, and felt in me the struggle of my motherland for awakening in spiritual emancipation. Our endeavours after political agitation seemed to me unreal to the core and pitifully feeble in their utter helplessness. I felt that it is a blessing of providence that begging should be an unprofitable profession and that only he who hath to him shall be given. I said to myself that we must seek for our own inheritance and with it buy our true place in the world.

Then came to me a vision of the fulness of the inner man which was attained in India in the solemn seclusion of her forests when the rest of the world was hardly awake. The truth became clear to me that India had cut her path and broadened it for ages, the path that leads to a life reaching beyond death, rising high above the idealisation of the political selfishness and insatiable lust for accumulation of materials. The voice came to me in the Vedic tongue from the *ashrams*, the forest sanctuaries of the past, with the call—"Come to me as the rivers to the sea, as the days and nights to the completion of their annual cycle. Let our taking and imparting truth be full of the radiance of light. Let us never come into conflict with one another. Let our minds speed towards their supreme good."

My heart responded to that call and I determined to do what I could to bring to the surface, for our daily use and purification the stream of ideals that originated in the summit of our past, flowing underground in the depth of India's soil,—the ideals of simplicity of life, clarity of spiritual vision, purity of heart, harmony with the universe, and consciousness of the infinite personality in all creation.

I knew that the lessons of the modern schools and the tendencies of the present time were aggressively antagonistic to these ideals, but also I was certain that the ancient teachers of India were true when they said with a positive assurance:—"It is an absolute death to depart from this life without realising the Eternal Truth of life."

Thus the exclusiveness of my literary life burst its barriers coming into touch with the deeper aspirations of my country lying hidden in her heart. I came to live in the Shantiniketan sanctuary founded by my father and there gradually gathered round me, under the shades of *sal* trees, boys from distant homes.

This was the time when Satish Chandra Roy, the author of the following little story, felt attracted to me and to my ideas and devoted himself to building up of the ashram and serving the boys with living food from the fulness of his life. He was barely nineteen, but he was born with a luminosity of soul. In him the spirit of renunciation was a natural product of an extraordinary capacity for enjoyment of life. All his student days he had been struggling with poverty—and yet he cheerfully gave up all chances of worldly prospects when they were near at hand and took his place in the ashram because it was truly his by right. He would have needed no recommendation from me, but unfortunately he died young before he had time to fulfil his promise, leaving the record of his greatness only in the memory of his friends.

I cannot but conclude this preface of mine with an extract from my lecture about Shantiniketan where I have described his connection with the ashram.

"Fortunately for me, Satish Chandra Roy, a young student of great promise, who was getting ready for his B. A. degree, became attracted to my school and devoted his life to carry out my idea. He was barely nineteen but he had a wonderful soul, living in a world of ideas, keenly responsive to all that was beautiful and great in the realm of nature and of human mind. He was a poet who would surely have taken his place among the immortals of the world-literature if he had lived, but he died when he was twenty, thus offering his service to our school only for the period of one short year. With

him boys never felt that they were confined in
the limits of a teaching class, they seemed to
have their access to everywhere. They would
go with him to the forest when in the spring the
sal trees were in full blossom, and he would recite
to them his favourite poems, frenzied with ex-
citement. He used to read to them Shakespeare
and even Browning—for he was a great lover of
Browning—explaining to them in Bengali with
his wonderful power of expression. He never
had any feeling of distrust for the boys' capacity
of understanding; he would talk and read to
them about whatever was the subject in which
he himself was interested. He knew that it
was not at all necessary for the boys to understand literally and accurately but that their
minds should be roused, and in this he was
always successful. He was not like other teachers, a mere vehicle of text books. He made his
teaching personal, he himself was the source of
it, and therefore it was made of life stuff easily
assimilable by the living human nature. The

real reason of his successes was his intense interest in life, in ideas, in everything around
him, in the boys who came in contact with him.
He had his inspiration not through the medium
of books but through the direct communication
of his sensitive mind with the world.   The seasons had upon him the same effect as they had
upon the plants.   He seemed to feel in his
blood the unseen messages of nature that are
always travelling through space, floating in the
air, shimmering in the leaves, tingling in the
roots of the grass under the earth.   The literature that he studied had not the least smell of
the library about it.   He had the power to see
ideas before him, as he could see his friends, with
all the distinctness of form and subtlety of life."

SHANTINIKETAN

BY

W. W. PEARSON

SHANTINIKETAN

W. W. PEARSON

The author of the story that follows was so intimately connected with the life of Rabindranath Tagore's school at Shantiniketan, Bolpur, that in order to understand the spirit of the story which was written for the boys of the ashram and was told them as they sat under the trees in the moonlight, a short account of the School itself seems a fitting introduction.

As our first impressions of a place are often the truest I will begin by an account of my first visit to Bolpur in 1912.

Bolpur is situated about a hundred miles from Calcutta so that the School is remote from the distractions of town life, and yet within easy reach of the stimulating activities of an intellectual centre. When I arrived at the station it was just sunset, the time picturesquely called in Bengal, the "cow dust" time, for it is then that the cattle are driven from the fields, and the sun sets behind a golden mist raised by the cows as they slowly make their way across the dusty fields. I was met by one of the masters and four of the older boys who took all my luggage from the carriage and carried it to the cart which was waiting outside the station. They welcomed me very warmly because I had just returned from England, where I had seen their Guru, and as we drove slowly along in the bullock cart our talk was chiefly about him. As we approached the School, which stands on high ground, so that the lights shine out over the surrounding country, one or two remarks, such as "That is one of his favourite walks" and

"Under those trees he often walks on moonlight nights," gave me the feeling that I was a pilgrim visiting the shrine of a saint rather than a visitor to a School. We became silent then, and no one spoke again till we reached the balcony of the guest house. There I was told the poet had written many of his songs. The evening star had just risen and a crescent moon was shedding its faint light over the tops of the trees with which the school is surrounded. Two of the boys went with me onto the roof and after singing one of the poet's songs, left me to spend a quiet evening with the master who had met me at the station. He helped me to realize the true spirit of the place, for he had been one of the five boys who had read in the school when it was first started. After a College course in America he had come back to devote his life to the service of the School to which he owed so much. We talked on about the ideals with which the poet had started the School. The sound of the boys' voices, as they came back from

THE POET'S UPPER ROOM

their evening meal to their dormitories, had
ceased, when in the stillness there arose the
sound of singing. It was a group of boys who,
every evening before they retire to bed, sing
one of the poet's songs. Gradually they
approached the house where we were sitting,
and as they turned away, the sound receded,
getting fainter and fainter until it died out
altogether. Then silence descended like shadows
on a starlit hill, and I realised why the name
"Shantiniketan" had been given to the place.
A House of Peace, it certainly was.

In the morning before sunrise, the band of young choristers wakened the sleeping school boys to the work of the day by another song.

After an early walk to a neighbouring village, where some of the older students conduct a night school for the boys of the Santal aboriginal tribes who are to be found scattered about in the neighborhood, I attended service in the temple, a building open to the light and air on all sides. As I entered, the boys in their coloured shawls were seated, some on the steps

THE SAL AVENUE

outside, and some on the white marble floor in an attitude of meditation. After an opening prayer in Bengali, the boys, all together, chanted a Sanskrit verse, ending with the words,

"Om, Shanti, Shanti, Shanti." "Om Peace, Peace
Peace."

To hear for the first time a Sanskrit prayer chanted by the boys of Bolpur is an experience not easily to be forgotten. I wish it were possible to preserve the freshness of one's first impressions, for then the very sound of the prayer would be a constant and never failing inspiration. I cannot describe the thrill which I felt as I listened to that ascending chant filling the fresh morning air with its solemn notes of youthful aspiration.

In the temple there is no image and no altar, for the Maharshi Devendranath Tagore who founded the ashram, declared that in Shantiniketan no image was to be worshipped and no abuse of any religious faith was to be allowed. There "the one invisible God is to be worshipped, and such instructions are to be given as are consistent with the worship, the praise, and the contemplation of the Creator and Maintainer of the world, and as are productive of good morals, religious life, and universal brotherhood."

The service was short, consisting only of the prayers and an address given by one of the teachers, but it was most impressive and devotional in spirit. The clear sunlight streamed through the screen of trees which surround the temple, and outside one could hear the chirping of birds, and distant cooing of doves.

During the day I came to know others of the teachers, and listened to some of the boys singing, for the poet's songs occupy a large part of the school life. The influence of Mr. Dinendranath Tagore, a nephew of the poet's, who teaches the boys the new songs as they are composed by the poet, is one the effect of which cannot be measured. To be able to spread the spirit of song is a great gift, but when together with it one is able to spread the ideals of a great spiritual teacher then the gift is one precious beyond words.

In the evening as it was a moonlight night, we went out, boys and teachers as well, to a wood about a mile away from the School. We sat in a circle under the trees and the boys sang. One of the teachers told a story, and I told them about my meeting with the poet in London. Then we walked back across the open country which lay still and quiet under the spell of the Indian moonlight.

The morning I left there was a farewell ceremony according to the ancient Hindu custom when a guest leaves an ashram for the outer world. I was garlanded and a handful of rose petals, together with some grains of paddy and some grass, symbolic of the plenitude and fruitfulness of life, was offered to me, and at the same time one of the teachers pronounced over me the blessing which is found in the Sanskrit "Sakuntala" and which has been translated by the poet, "Pleasant be thy path with intervals of cool lakes green with the spreading leaves of lotus, and with the shady trees tempering the glare and heat of the sun—let its dust be gentle for you even like the pollen of flowers borne by the calm and friendly breeze—let your path be auspicious."

That I felt was my dedication to the service of the ashram, and as I left for the station I knew that my life work lay in trying to help to realise the ideals for which the ashram stood. There I knew was an atmosphere in which self-realisation was possible and a place where I could feel the throbbing heart of Bengal, the land of poetry and imagination.

Since then I have lived in the ashram, I have got to know the boys and the teachers as my friends for life, I have felt, even when my own spirit has been dull and I have not been able to feel the same inspiration as I hear the boys chanting in the early morning or at sunset, that Shantiniketan is truly an Abode of Peace.

Now that I am away from the ashram for a time my thoughts constantly turn back to it, and I know that under that wide and starry sky, wandering across the open heath which stretches to the horizon on all sides so that one feels as if standing on the roof of the world, there is peace to be found for the restless spirit of man. On nights when the full moon sheds a flood of white peace upon the landscape one can walk for miles across open country with nothing to obstruct the view except here and there a neat Santal village surrounded by its few cultivated fields, and on the distant line of the horizon a group of tall palm trees standing like the warning fore-fingers of the guardian spirits of the place, raised against all thoughtless curiosity of outside in-trusions. As one lives in this ashram and ab-sorbs the spirit of its founder, one feels that its stillness and peace are but the reflection of the tranquility which filled the mind of the Maharshi

BOYS AT AN EXAMINATION

THE SMALL BOY'S DORMITORIES

Devendranath and is so marked a characteristic
of the poet.   In the evenings and early mornings, just at sunset and sunrise, when the school
bell has called the boys to their silent worship,
a silence strangely still and beautiful seems to
surround the place; and in the early hours of the
morning, long before the peep of light in the
east, the stillness is so intense that it seems as if
time has held its breath in the expectation of the
daily wonder of the sunrise.

Does it seem as if this ashram were too remote
and monastic for the training of boys who, when
they leave school, have to struggle in the modern
world? Can we not say rather, that perhaps
here they may acquire what the modern world
most needs, that wealth of mind's tranquility
which is required to give life its balance when
it has to march to its goal through the crowd of
distractions? Whatever may be the practical
outcome of this experiment in education, which
strives to combine the best traditions of the old
Hindu system of teaching with the healthiest

aspects of modern methods, there can be no
doubt that the ideal is a high one.   Let me tell
more of what these ideals are and how the boys
and teachers of the school strive to carry them
into practice.

Shantiniketan was originally a bare spot in
the middle of open country, and was notorious
for being the haunt of dacoits.   It was to this
spot that Maharshi Devendranath came on one
of his journeys, and he was so deeply attracted
to the place that he pitched his tent under three
trees, which were the only trees then to be seen
there, and for weeks at a time would live there
spending his time in meditation and prayer.
These trees are still to be seen, with the wide
open plain stretching out before them to the
Western horizon, and on the marble slab which
marks the place of his meditation can be seen
the words which filled his mind as the Maharshi
meditated upon God.

> "He is the repose of my life
>   the joy of my heart,
>   the peace of my spirit."

It is under these trees that the boys sometimes meet when they commemorate the life of the Maharshi, or others whose lives have bound them close to the heart of the ashram. I remember the last meeting which I attended there. It was early morning and the boys were all seated in the shade of the trees which were a mass of white blossom overhead. The bright colours of their shawls as the sunlight fell through the interlacing branches contrasted with the white flowers above them, and in perfect silence they waited for the service to begin.

This custom of holding meetings out of doors is characteristic of the school, where all the classes are held under the trees or in the verandahs, excepting during the Rains. The boys often organise some entertainment in the evenings, some circus performance or small play composed by the boys themselves, to which the masters are invited. Just before I left for America the smaller boys had discovered the existence of an imaginary hero named Ladam,

and for several days the history of Ladam occu-
pied their minds. Pictures were drawn of his
exploits, his heroic deeds, some of them by no
means exemplary, were staged for the benefit
of their teachers, and every tree and hillock in
the neighborhood of the small boys' dormitories
was made the scene of Ladam's fights and vic-
tories. I was shown an ant hill and was told
that it was the fortress of Ladam, and that the
ants were his disciples and followers. Since
my last acquaintance of him, whether Ladam
has come to an end of his career of reckless and
inconsequential adventures, I know not, but as
long as he lived his friends and discoverers were
never tired of telling of his deeds and describing
with the minutest details his appearance and
character. Perhaps his ghost still haunts the
corners of the dormitory and the shadow-
chequered path of the Sal avenue.

This characteristic of one side of the school
life is vital to the ideals with which the school
was started. Education consists, not in giving

information which the boys will forget as soon
as they conveniently can without danger of
failing in their examinations, but in allowing
the boys to develop their own characters in the
way which is natural to them. The younger the
boys are the more original they show themselves
to be. It is only when the shadow of a Uni-
versity examination begins to loom over them
that they lose their natural freshness and orig-
inality, and become candidates for matricul-
ation. When the small boys take up an
idea and try to put it into practice then there is
always a freshness about it which is spontaneous
and full of the joy of real creation. To see them
give a circus performance would delight the
heart of any man who had not become absolutely blasé.

This ideal of allowing the boys to develop
their own characters as much as possible is seen
in another institution of the school, namely the
Courts constituted by the boys for the punish-
ment of minor offences against the laws which

the boys themselves formulate. Most of the discipline of the school is managed by these courts, and although there are doubtless cases of miscarriage of justice, there is no complaint amongst the boys about the judgments pronounced against offenders. In this case as in others, self-government is better than good government. The committees which the boys form are intended to deal with all the aspects of the school life in which the boys are themselves vitally interested. On one occasion the boys agreed to carry on all the menial work of the school, cooking and washing up, drawing the water and buying the stores, with the help of the teachers. And although the experiment was only found practicable for about a month, during that time there were no servants employed to do any of this heavy work, and many of the boys worked like Trojans without complaint even though it was the very hottest time of the year.

There are several magazines published monthly by the different sections of the school, most of them in Bengali, which contain stories, poems and essays written by the boys. These are illustrated by those of them who show signs of artistic ability. Though these magazines sometimes languish, and often do not appear for months together, they quicken into life when the anniversary of their birth comes round, and then a grand celebration takes place. One of the dormitories is taken possession of for the occasion, and decorated with the green branches of trees, and if it happens to be the season of lotuses, a profusion of lotus buds and blossoms fills the meeting place. One of the teachers is elected to be the chairman for the evening, and a special seat of honour is prepared for him. Over his head there hang, like the sword of Damocles, ropes of flowers, so that he looks like a queen of the May, and round his neck hang garlands as though he were a lamb prepared for the sacrifice. The various committees of management of these different periodicals vie with each other, not so much in the quality of their contributions, as in the beauty of the decorations and the garlands which are prepared in honour of these occasions of birthday celebration. Sometimes if the anniversary happens to fall during the hot weather, light refreshments are served at the close of the meeting, generally in the shape of iced sherbet. The meeting itself consists of a report of the year's progress by the editor, and the reading of stories, poems and essays by the contributors. Sometimes pictures which have been given for illustration are exhibited, and afterwards the chairman or the poet himself, if he is present, will criticise the writings which have been read, suggesting in what way they might be improved. In certain cases there is a competition, either for the best picture or the best story. In this way the boys are encouraged to think and write for themselves, and one or two of those who have illustrated these manuscript magazines have proved to be artists of real ability.

Occasionally excursions will be planned, either for the day for the whole school, or for several days to some place of historical interest in which case only a few selected boys will go accompanied by two or three of the teachers. In the former case we go to some place within easy reach of the ashram, and taking our food with us cook it by the side of a river or under the trees in a wood. The whole day is spent in the open air, and singing and games form the chief part of the program though stories are also told by some of the teachers. On moonlight nights, especially, many of the boys go out for long walks with the teachers, and in this way the bond between the masters and the pupils becomes deep and strong. The teachers live in the dormitories with the boys, and are able therefore to help them in their work and share with them their daily life.

Football is the most popular form of sport in the school, and as there is plenty of space round the buildings, there is enough ground for several football fields, so that the boys of all ages can have their own games. Walking is not so popular, except when, in the rainy season sudden storms of rain come deluging the surrounding country. Then the boys delight in going out into the midst of the heaviest deluge and getting thoroughly wet. Classes are stopped when these heavy storms come on, and keen delight is shown by the boys when they see that a dark and threatening sky offers them the chance of a cooling shower bath.

The following facts may be of interest to those who wish to know the more practical details of the working of the School.

At present there are about 150 boys in the ashram, some of whom come from other parts of India, though the majority are from Bengal. There are about twenty teachers, some living with their families, resident in the School. The age of the boys ranges from six to 17 or 18, the younger ones being under the charge of special teachers. These younger boys often take their meals in the homes of the married teachers, the wife of one of them, for example, having undertaken to look after ten boys who come to her house for all their meals for a week, allowing another ten to take their turn.

The boys are of all castes and it is expressly stated when they are admitted that they are to be allowed to exercise their own discretion in the matter of the observation or non-observation of caste distinctions. Serving at the meals is undertaken by all the boys in turn which lightens the burden of the kitchen service.

The fees charged are the same for all the boys, though in certain cases poor students are allowed free. Each pupil is charged $7 per month for tuition, board and lodging, so that the yearly expense to the parent is less than $100. But this does not represent the actual expense, as there is a large yearly deficit which has, up to the present, been met by the founder of the School.

One of the reasons which makes it impossible to make the School a self-supporting institution is that the number of teachers has to be so large in proportion to the number of students in order to ensure small classes and individual attention.

To the Western eye the outward aspect of the School would suggest poverty, but this is due to the ideal which has always been followed in India wherever true education has been the end and purpose in view. The emphasis on efficient and expensive equipment which is a characteristic feature of institutions of learning in the West has never been accepted in India where simplicity of living is regarded as one of the most important factors in true education.

The utmost simplicity is found in all the buildings which are used by the boys for their own daily life. The dormitories are merely thatched cottages, and it is intended to keep them simple though the present thatched roofs will have to be changed for a less inflammable material as soon as funds are available, as the possibility of a fire which would spread to all the dormitories is a source of constant anxiety.

We are hoping to erect a new building for a Hospital, as we have not proper accommodation for our sick boys or suitable quarters for the segregation of infectious cases. Such a hospital, when properly endowed, would provide medical help for the poor of the neighbouring villages. Several interesting collections of curios from different parts of the world have been presented to the School, and we intend to add a Museum as an addition to the present library building as soon as funds are forthcoming.

The daily routine of the School is as follows: The boys are awakened before sunrise by the singing of one of the poet's songs by a band of singers. As soon as they get up they go to their morning bath which they take by the wells which have been sunk in different parts of the grounds. After their bath they have fifteen minutes set apart for silent worship. The boys sit out under the trees or on the open fields in the early morning light and then come together to chant the Sanskrit verses selected from the Upanishads by Maharshi Debendranath Tagore.

After some light food the classes begin at about seven o'clock. There are no classrooms, so the classes are held in the open air or on the verandahs of the buildings.

After a meal at 11:30, during the heat of the day the boys stay in their rooms and work at their lessons, the teachers sitting with them to give help if needed. Classes begin in the afternoon at 2 o'clock and continue till 4:30 or 5 o'clock.

In the cool of the evening football is played, while some of the boys go for walks. At sunset they have fifteen minutes for silence and the chanting of the evening verses. Some of the boys teach in a night school which has been started for the servants of the School and the neighbouring villagers.

Before the evening meal there is an hour which is devoted to some form of entertainment, such as story telling by one of the teachers, a lantern lecture, or some amusement got up by the boys themselves. The bell for retiring sounds at about nine o'clock, and most of the boys are asleep by 9:30, except on moonlight nights when numbers of the older boys go out for a walk to neighbouring woods where they sit and sing till late at night.

There is no head master, the school being under the management of an executive committee elected by the teachers themselves, from among whom one is elected each year as executive head. He is entrusted with the practical management of the institution. In each subject one of the masters is elected as director of studies, and he discusses with the other teachers in that subject the books and methods of teaching to be adopted, but each teacher is left to work out his own methods in the way he thinks best.

When the poet is himself present he presides at the meetings of the executive committee, and also teaches in some of the classes, but his influence is more widely felt in the informal readings of his own writings which he gives in the evenings during the entertainment period. He also teaches the boys, when they take part in his plays, not only how to act but also how to sing his songs.

The boys are trusted very largely to look after their own affairs, and have their own committees in the different sections of the School, as well as the general meetings of all the boys in the ashram when questions affecting the whole School are brought up for discussion. In their examinations they are left to themselves and put on their honour. When an examination takes place the boys may be seen in all sorts of positions writing their answers, even in such inacessible places as the fork of some high tree. Though occasionally boys take advantage of the trust thus placed in them it is found that in the majority of cases trust begets trust, and there is no question that the relationship between teacher and pupil is a happier one in consequence.

The old boys of the ashram keep in touch with the school in different ways. The boys who are in the ashram know these "old boys" by the title of "Dada," which means elder brother, and at the annual festival, which takes place in December on the anniversary of the date on which the ashram was founded, numbers of the old boys come to see the performance of one of the poet's plays.   The keenest interest is taken by all in the football match between Past and Present Boys.   The School is not behind-hand in Sports as can be seen by its record in the inter-school Sports of the district in which boys from our ashram have carried off the chief prizes for several years in succession.   Their football record also is one to be proud of, so the education of the boys includes physical culture as well as culture of the mind.

As I have said, the classes are held in the open air as much as possible, and there is no need for elaborate furniture and class rooms.   Each boy brings with him to the various classes his own square piece of carpet for sitting on, and the teacher either sits under a tree, or in the verandah of one of the dormitories.   This open air class work has its great advantages, for it keeps the minds of the boys fresh in their appreciation of nature. I remember in the middle of one class I was suddenly interrupted in my teaching by one of the boys calling my attention to the song of a bird in the branches overhead. We stopped the teaching and listened till the bird had finished. It was spring time and the boy who had called my attention to the song said to me, "I don't know why, but somehow I can't explain what I feel when I hear that bird singing." I could not enlighten him, but I am quite sure that my class learnt more from that bird than it had ever done from my teaching, and something that they would never forget in life. For myself my ears were opened and for several days I was conscious of the songs of the birds as I had never been before. The boys are very fond of flowers and some times will get up long before dawn to be the first to pluck some new sweet-scented blossoms. These they weave into garlands for their teachers or for the poet himself.

Sometimes when the class comes at the end of the day, the boys ask that they may go out to some neighboring village or the river, and have the class on the way. When this happens then they are supremely happy, and we go off together with no other anxiety than that of getting back in time for the evening meal.

For the younger boys Nature Study forms part of their work, and during the whole of one term one class was kept busy in collecting all the varieties of leaves and grasses that could be found in the neighborhood. Sometimes they would find an unexpected addition to their collection of botanical specimens, by getting a thorn into their bare feet, for all the boys go about barefoot in the ashram. But their feet are so hardened to the gravel and thorny paths which abound all round the school that it is only the new boys that find any hardship in such an experience. Occasionally on a clear night one of the teachers gives a simple lesson in astronomy, and shows the moon and stars through a small telescope, and when lantern slides can be obtained illustrated lectures are given in the evenings, sometimes in the open air and sometimes in one of the dormitories. It is always possible to find one or two of the more practical boys eager to take charge of the lantern, and fix up the sheet.

Bengali is the medium of instruction throughout the School, but English is taught as a second language.

The direct method of teaching English is adopted in the lower classes, and when the boys are beginning to understand, fairy stories or adventures are told to the boys in simple English. When the boys are interested in a story it is surprising with what ease they are able to follow. I have myself found such stories as George Macdonald's "The Princess and Curdie" and "The Princess and the Goblins" fascinate Bengali boys of thirteen or fourteen, and they have been eager to hear the next instalment, even though told them in a foreign language.

One of the things that strikes visitors to the school is the look of happiness on the boys' faces, and there is no doubt that there is none of the usual feeling of dislike for school life which one finds in institutions where the only object held before the boys is the passing of examinations. Examinations have been abolished in the lower classes, except once a year when tests of each boy's progress are made by the teacher who has been teaching the boy himself.

At the end of each term arrangements are made for staging one of the poet's plays. The teachers and boys take the different parts, and the play is staged in Shantiniketan, visitors coming from Calcutta to see it, especially if the poet is himself taking part. The poet coaches the actors himself, first reading the play aloud, and then reading it over with those who are to take part. During the days when the play is being rehearsed there are not many classes held, for the boys of the whole school are always present at the rehearsals. One sees the small boys peeping in at the windows, and showing the keenest appreciation of the humourous and witty scenes. The final day is a busy one for the stage has to be prepared and there must be a dress rehearsal. To this the boys are not admitted, as it would take away the freshness of the play if they were able to see a too nearly perfect presentation of it beforehand. But when it begins there is great enthusiasm amongst visitors and boys alike, as the songs and dances reveal the spirit of the play to the delighted audience. In this way the ideas of the poet are assimilated by the boys, without their having to make any con-scious effort. In fact they are being educated into his thought through the sub-conscious mind, and this is one of the root principles of Rabindranath Tagore's method of education. English plays are also sometimes given, as well

as Sanskrit, and it is remarkable to see what
histrionic powers the Bengali boy has, even when
he has to act in a foreign tongue. When the
play is in Bengali then they are in their element,
and they seem to have such aptitude for acting
that the smaller boys often get up plays of their
own without any assistance from the masters.
At the beginning of this year there was a performance of the poet's new play "A Spring
Festival" in Calcutta, and a number of the
younger boys, aged from eight to ten, took
part in the chorus. They did not have to do
any acting, but merely sang the songs and took
part in the dances, so that they were practically
in the position of spectators on the stage. After
the play was over, and we had all returned to
Shantiniketan, these small boys surprised us by
giving one evening a performance of the whole
play, each boy taking one of the characters with
such perfect mimicry of those who had taken
the parts in Calcutta that the performance
was irresistible. Every shade of humour and

seriousness was reproduced to perfection by these pigmy actors.

An account of the school would be incomplete without some reference to what strike one as the peculiar characteristics of the Bengali boys as distinguished from English boys. In the grounds of the school there is a small Hospital building in which the boys when ill reside, and to which outdoor patients from the surrounding villages come for treatment. There is a qualified doctor in charge but the nursing is done almost entirely by the boys themselves, who in the case of the serious illness of one of their schoolfellows, divide the night up into watches of two hours each, and look after the patient all night. They seem to have a natural instinct which makes them splendid nurses even when they have not had any special training. It is not only towards the boys themselves that they show this care, but when necessity arises for helping some poor villager from the neighborhood they will go to the village, and perhaps carry the patient on a stretcher to the school hospital in order that he may get proper treatment.

The story of Jadav well illustrates this remarkable spirit. Jadav was one of the boys in the lower part of the School. He was only about eleven years old but he was a brilliant boy and full of promise. He was taken ill while he was with us and died in the ashram.

I remember so well his keen interest in Nature Study, and how he would come running and panting to my class with his latest addition to the collections of different kinds of leaves which the smaller boys were making. His words tumbling over each other in his eagerness to show me what treasures he had found, he would ask me whether any other boy had got so many different kinds. All his teachers found in him the same eager interest in his work, and at meetings of the smaller boys he would sometimes tell a story in English which was wonderfully good for so young a pupil.

When he was first taken ill it was not realised that it was anything serious, but after a week or so he became worse and it was decided to remove him to Calcutta as the accommodation in our small Hospital building was not satisfactory for cases of serious illness. Many of the older boys had been taking their turns in sitting up at night with the little patient, and when the morning came for him to be removed eight or ten of them took up the stretcher on which he was to be carried to the station and started off along the road. As soon as Jadav realised that he was being taken away to Calcutta his whole body became restless and instead of lying still and quiet in his weakness he began to struggle and cry out, "I don't want to leave the ashram. Take me back." "I won't go. I want to go back to the ashram." "Why are you taking me away?"

The doctor became alarmed and said that it would be dangerous to take him if he struggled and cried, so the boys turned back towards the ashram again. The moment he realised that he was returning to his ashram the little fellow lay quite still and he was happy again.

He began to get worse however and in spite of the best medical aid that could be got from Calcutta it soon became clear that we were to lose his bright presence. Day after day the boys took their turns in watching by his side and carrying out the doctors' instructions and would sit up all through the night bathing his fevered body with cool water.

An hour or two before he died I was sitting by his side and he said in Bengali in a voice weak and full of pathos, "The flower will not blossom." I whispered to him, "Don't be afraid, for the flower will blossom."

He was cremated out on the open fields near the ashram at dawn and as the flames crept slowly upwards I knew that for us at least his little life had blossomed and left a fragrance behind which would never fade.

Another striking characteristic of the Bengali boy is his genuine affection for little children. The average English boy, if told to take charge of an infant brother would feel completely miserable, and if asked to carry his baby sister to the Annual Prize Giving of his own school would feel ready to sink through the floor with shame. But in Bengali wherever one goes he is struck by the fact that the boys are devoted to children and are never tired of nursing them or playing with them. I have seen boys at Shantiniketan spend hours wheeling a perambulator with quite a young child in it for the mere pleasure of having a child to entertain. There is no affectation about it, and this is not a peculiarity of the boys of our school only. Nothing gives the boys of the upper classes at Shantiniketan more pleasure than to be allowed to bring to their class the grandson of the poet, a little boy of four who sits through the period quite quietly and solemnly, with only an occasional diversion if anything interesting is happening near the tree

under which the class is being held.   And I have
often seen one of the biggest boys, on the way
to the football field, hand in hand with the tiny
son of one of the teachers, a little boy of three,
who chatters away to his big companion on all
sorts of subjects.

Bengali boys have also a characteristic attitude of receptivity to spiritual things which
makes it possible to trust to the atmosphere of
the ashram for the development of the spiritual
life.   There is, for example, nothing irksome to
the boys in the habit of sitting in silence and
stillness during the morning and evening periods
of silent worship.   The result of this is that even
the younger boys of our school often find it
easier to follow the addresses of the poet than
graduate students of Calcutta, who have not
had the opportunity of living in such an en-
vironment.   They are like sensitive instruments
which respond to the least influence, and for that
reason unkindness or thoughtlessness in one's
dealings with Bengali students often have

results apparently far out of proportion to the actual occasion of the hurt. This has been seen recently in the effect of an unsympathetic attitude adopted by many professors in Government and other Colleges towards the students in Calcutta. But this very sensitiveness responds with even greater readiness to kindness and sympathy. In educational work of any kind sympathy is the supreme necessity for a successful teacher, but this is truer in Bengal than in any other country in the world.

Before closing some reference should be made to the religious atmosphere of the place. I say religious *atmosphere* because there is no definite dogmatic teaching, and for the development of the spiritual side of the boys' natures the ideal has always been to leave that to the natural instinct of each individual boy. In this considerable help is expected from the personal influence of the teachers, and in the silent but constant influence of close touch with Nature

herself, which in India is the most wonderful
teacher of spiritual truth.

Shantiniketan was founded by the father of
the poet, Maharshi Devendranath Tagore, as
an ashram, or religious retreat where those in
search of peace might have an opportunity for
quiet and meditation, and when Rabindranath
chose it as the site for his school he knew that
the atmosphere of the place was an ideal one for
the growth of his own ideals. The eldest son of
the Maharshi, Mr. Dwijendranath Tagore has
also chosen this place for the closing years of his
life, and is still living there in his seventy-fifth
year, spending his days in quiet meditation and
writing on religious and philosophical subjects.
On the first day of the New Year, and on other
special occasions, all the boys and teachers go
to pay their reverence to this saint who has now
lived constantly for about twenty years in
Shantiniketan, and is as much a vital part of
the ashram as the boys themselves. One of the
rarest privileges is that of going in the evening

to his house and in the fading twilight to sit and talk with him on the deeper things of the spirit.

Mention has been made of the period set apart in the early morning and evening for meditation. Each boy takes his piece of carpet out into the open field or under a tree when the bell for worship sounds, and sits there for fifteen minutes in silent contemplation, or perhaps one should say in silence, for the subject of his thoughts is left entirely to each boy. There is no instruction given as to the method of meditation, the direction of their thoughts being left to the influence of the idea of silence itself and to the Sanskrit texts which are repeated by the boys together at the close of the period of silent meditation. That many boys form the habit of such daily silent worship is enough. Apart from this morning and evening silence there is a service held in the temple once or twice a week at which the poet himself, when present, addresses the boys. When he is away one of the teachers gives the address, and the boys join in the chanting of

certain Sanskrit mantras. The subject of these
addresses varies, and many of them have been
published in a series entitled "Shantiniketan,"
which have been published by the school authori-
ties. As an example I may give the notes I took
of an address given by the poet on the last night
of the old year. The service was held after sunset and in the darkness it was only possible to
distinguish the speaker dimly outlined against a
background of white clad figures seated on the
floor all round him.

He began by saying that when a year comes
to its end we sometimes think only of the sad-
ness of ending, but if we can realise that in this
ending there is not emptiness but fulness, then
even the thought of ending itself becomes full of
joy. In this very process of ending we once
again have the leisure to throw off the coverings
and wrappings of habit and custom and thus
emerge into a fuller and more spacious conception
of life. Even the ending of life in death has this
element of fulness in it when viewed from the

right standpoint.   Death really reveals life to us
and never hides or obscures it except where we
ourselves are wilfully blind.   Thus the breaking
of customs and forms which have grown round
us only to choke true life is a matter for joy and
not sorrow.   In Europe this war, which is
robbing so many homes by death, is really the
tearing off, on a vast scale, of the wrappings of
dead habits of mind which have been accumu-
lating for so many years only to smother the
truth of our nature.   The currents of life which
had become choked and stagnant will once more
become free to flow in fresh channels.

When death comes to those whom we love,
we seem to see the world in its completeness, but
without the customary crowd of things which
hide from us the reality underlying the scene.
In death's presence the world becomes like the
darkness which is so full that one feels it can be
pierced with a needle and yet it seems empty of
objects.

Thus the message of this end of the year is the joy of change and its acceptance as the means of achieving a wider vision and grasp of life.

The address was full of illuminating illustrations as all the poet's addresses are, and I have only given the barest outline of this one in order to give some idea of the kind of subjects which are taken. The fact that some of them seem to be above the heads of the boys does not seriously matter, for the boys, even without fully understanding, are all the time unconsciously absorbing the point of view of the speaker.

In closing I cannot do better than quote in full a letter written to a Schoolmaster in England who had written to the poet asking for an account of the methods he adopts at Shantiniketan. He writes:

"To give spiritual culture to our boys was my principal object in starting my school in Bolpur. Fortunately, in India we have the model before us in the tradition of our ancient forest schools where teachers whose aim was to realise their lives in God had their homes. The atmosphere was full of the aspiration for the infinite, and the students who grew up with their teachers closely united with them in spiritual relationship felt the reality of God— for it was no mere creed imposed upon them or speculative abstraction.

Having this ideal of a school in my mind which should be a home and a temple in one, where teaching should be part of a worshipful life I selected this spot, away from all distractions of town, hallowed by the memory of a pious life whose days were passed there in communion with God.

You must not imagine that I have fully realised my ideal—but the ideal is there working itself out through all the obstacles of the hard prose of modern life. In spiritual matters one should forget that he must teach others or achieve results that can be measured, and in my school here I think it proper to measure our success by the spiritual growth in the teachers.

In these things gain to one's personal self is gain to all, like lighting a lamp which is lighting a whole room.

The first help that our boys get here on this path, is from the cultivation of love of nature and sympathy with all living creatures. Music is of very great assistance to them—songs being not of the ordinary hymn type, dry and didactic, but as full of lyric joy as the author could put in them. You can understand how these songs affect the boys when you know that singing them is the best enjoyment they choose for themselves in their leisure time, in the evening when the moon is up, in the rainy days when their classes are closed. Mornings and evenings fifteen minutes time is given them to sit in an open space composing their minds for worship. We never watch them and ask questions about what they think in those times, but leave it entirely to themselves, to the spirit of the place and the time, and the suggestion of the practice itself. We rely more upon the subconscious influence of Nature, of the associations of the place and the daily life of worship that we live than on any conscious effort to teach them."

This letter sums up better than I can the ideals of Shantiniketan and gives expression to the spirit with which the ashram was started.

THE GIFT TO THE GURU

THE GIFT TO THE GURU

BY SATISH CHANDRA ROY

Translated by W. W. Pearson

Introduction

This evening I am going to tell you a story about a boy of long ago.

Forget for a while this lamp that we have lighted indoors, and think of that flood of moonlight that pours itself out upon the surrounding fields. On one side of this open country the wood is black and indistinct like a huge python that has risen from some chasm of the earth and is lying asleep in the moonlight, swaying in

the wind. To-night as we all sit together I
shall speak to you about the night. If it had
been daytime, perhaps I should have talked
about the day. But no,—I have another reason for describing the night, for night time is the
best time for story-telling. At night time everything seems indistinct and distant objects are
brought near. If it had been daytime, would
you have been able so easily to think that you
were seeing the stars, which, when the sky is
caressed by the shadow of the night, blossom
like flowers and fill the heavens in their multi-
tudes?

So far I have been describing the night, in
order to carry you in thought out into the
darkness, where the sky is decked with the
moon and stars. Now you must accompany
me in imagination wherever I go.

What journey shall we take together? We
are going to visit a sacred grove of ancient India.
If it had been day time, how could you ever
have discovered this sacred grove of hundreds of

years ago? If it had been day time, what should we have seen in modern India? We should have seen cities, railways and factories; we should have seen forests full of wild beasts, dried-up rivers, hard rocky mountains, barren parched deserts and many other things besides. The sacred grove I am to tell you about no longer exists.

But it is night time now—moonlight is falling and the silence of sleep has come. Now the mind can take wings and fly in imagination wherever it wishes. Come then let us forget everything and all go together to see the Ashram * of the Rishis† in that wood of ancient India. You are Brahmacharis‡ and you can for a time go with me and exchange thoughts with the Brahmacharies of those days.

---

* Ashram: A forest school where the teachers and their families live with the boys in some retired spot.

† Rishis: Saints.

‡ Brahmacharis: Students brought up to a life of discipline in an atmosphere of religion.

CHAPTER I

In olden times boys used to go for purposes of study to a Brahmachari-ashram. I have already told you that schools of that kind were situated in sacred groves. Rishis used to think that though it is necessary for groups of men to build cities in places where there is a great deal of business and bustle, yet there are other needs besides these, which human life is meant to fulfil.

If you live only in the busy work and turmoil of the world, you will not get time to understand, or even to see properly, all aspects of the world. The mind will have no peace; and if the mind is not tranquil, then the real meaning of things will not be understood, nor will their real beauty be appreciated.

Besides this there was another advantage in living in a forest, namely, that man felt a kind of freedom and was able to realise his own worth. Each one had to do his own work, so that no false ideas crept in, that such a one was poor, and therefore unimportant, and such a one was rich, and therefore great.

It was those forest saints who were really able to uphold the ideals of India, which made peace and tranquility the greatest of blessings. In the solitudes of these forests, and in the midst of the beauty of these woods, the teaching given had a deep and penetrating effect. That was the reason why the students of those days saw such a wonderful glory in the world.

From the story that I am going to relate, you will be able to see what great strength a pupil gained from his training in a solitary place such as I have described.

So now I will begin my story.

CHAPTER II

One day, when it was just dawn in the sacred grove, Ved the Rishi of the Ashram, having finished his morning prayer and worship of the sacred fire called his pupils together, fresh from their morning bath, and sat with them at the foot of an Amloki tree.

The deer have now risen from their sleep in the courtyard and run into the forest. One of the boys has driven a cow into a meadow luscious with fresh tender grass.   Now as he sits under a tree the soft rays of the sun, falling through the cool green network of leaves and branches, light up his face and he is singing with a sweet low voice a hymn to the sun.   A band of younger boys with baskets in their hands are filling them with flowers from the woods.   Near by the wife of their Guru*, as she comes from the river, is pouring a little water from a pitcher on to the roots of each tree and smiles as she looks with tenderness at the boys.

Thus while the fresh calmness of early morning rests on the scene Ved begins to explain to the boys with a voice full of joy the sacred mysteries of God.   Gazing on the radiant face of their Guru the boys began to listen attentively.   When the morning reading was finished two or three deer came to the place where they were, and began to nestle with their warm

---

* Guru: Teacher and master.

breath and soft noses against the boys' bodies.
A few of the students however remained seated
in silent thought quite motionless.

Then one of the older boys, named Utonka,
came up and having bowed before his Guru's
feet said with clasped hands.

"To-day my time of discipline is finished. I
have by your love gained strength. My body
has become strong and my mind bright and
happy. I have seen the glory of the sun and
moon and have felt a Power in the glowing fire.
I have tasted the joys of the six seasons of the
year. The peace and tranquility of the forests
have taken up their abode in me and the fresh
living spirit of the birds and beasts, of the trees
and creepers, has entered my heart. I have
come to understand that the food which we eat
and the wood of the trees which we burn in the
fire are to be deemed sacred because they do us
good. Air, water, sky and light are sacred
also, and all are filled with divine sweetness and
goodness.

"Gurudev, I have learnt to understand all this and now I must go out into the wider world. In that outer world there are hundreds and hundreds of men like me and my duty now lies amongst them, for man cannot live without human love. By your help, Gurudev, I have become a Brahmachari. My body is strong; I am not afraid of difficulties, and when I go out into the world I shall be able to fulfil my purpose by your blessing. My Guru, give me then your blessing, and tell me what offering I am to bring you. When I have made my offering, I will bid farewell."

While Utonka was speaking, all the other boys were watching him with sorrowful faces. Hearing that he was going away their eyes filled with tears. Gurudev also with tearful, yet smiling, eyes said,—"My son the heart of a Guru is always with his disciples, the blessings of a Guru are taken up by the clouds and fall like rain from heaven. They touch his eyes mingling with the light of the sun. Like the

breeze they waft their fragrance around him,
day by day, and dwell in his heart as peace and
tenderness.   You need not ask for my blessing:
it is yours already.   Go out into the world and
my blessing be with you.   What further offering can I desire, my son?   Go to your mother,
and if you can bring anything that she desires,
you will be free from your debt to your Guru."

Utonka replied,—"Gurudev, I cannot hope
ever to free myself from my debt to you, but,
I will do as you say, and will go and ask my
mother."   Saying this he threw himself at his
Guru's feet and then slowly went away.

The other pupils remained silent with sorrow
and the Guru also for a little time was silent.
At last he said, "My children, it it now time for
you to go and beg your food."   The boys making an obeisance to their Guru dispersed in all
directions, to beg from the village food for
themselves and their Guru.   Amongst them
there were the sons of many rich and influential
men but all of them begged without distinction.

CHAPTER III

Utonka then went to his teacher's wife who was sitting in the shade of a tree near the house weaving grass mats, a deer was lying beside her while overhead a bird was making a loud noise, "Tee tee ū, Tee tee ū" other smaller birds flying about without a care and drinking water from the pools under the Ashoka trees. It really seemed as if these birds and beasts were one with man.

After bowing before his teacher's wife, Utonka said, "Mother, the time of my training is finished and I have, by the help of Gurudev, become a Brahmachari. I have gained strength and now I must go into the world. Tell me

now, Mother, what offering I can make you:
for Gurudev told me to ask you."

Quickly putting aside her weaving his teacher's
wife said with tears in her eyes, "What! my child,
are you going to leave us? Yet why should I be
sad? Go take my blessing with you. How
many of my sons have one after another gone
away like this. But I am not sorrowful; for
from the ashram they go out into the world and
benefit it by their work. Can any one spend all
his life in the seclusion of this forest? But
wherever you go my heart's affection and blessing will surround you all your life."

Then after a short silence she said, "What
offering shall I tell you to bring? Though we
need nothing, we must observe the usual custom." Then as if remembering something she
said with a slight smile:

"I have just remembered something. The
Queen Shubashukla is famous all the world over.
Even the gods respect her virtue. The saints
of the forests sing her praises and even a hard

stone would be melted by the love of her generous heart. No impure person is allowed to look
upon her face. She has some golden ear-rings
which are so valuable that Takshat, the king of
the serpents, himself wants to keep them in his
storehouse in the nether regions. I have a great
desire to see and touch those ear-rings just
once, and I would like to wear them when next
I entertain the Brahmins. So bring me those
ear-rings within three days so that my wish may
be fulfilled. You are a Brahmachari and should
have no difficulty."

Utonka was delighted, and having saluted her
he determined to set off that very day to bring
his offering.

When he had gone, the Guru's wife sat still
and began to think to herself: "I wonder if I
have done right to send my child Utonka all
alone such a long distance to bring this offering.
But why should I be afraid? Let him see the
glory of a virtuous woman before he enters the
world. Why should one be afraid for a

Brahmachari?" As she thought in this fashion, she remembered all Utonka's deep devotion and goodness, and she began to feel sad.

By this time the other boys came back, bringing the rice and other food they had begged—but to-day strange to say, there was none of the chatter and happy noise which there was on other days. The Guru's wife seeing the boys looking so sad went up to them and asked them the cause. They all cried, "Utonka is going away." Then she went off towards the kitchen consoling them as she went.

CHAPTER IV

Now we must follow Utonka on his journey
to the palace of King Poshya, the husband of the
famous queen. After leaving the fields near the
ashram he entered a thick forest. It was
then midday, and the forest was very beautiful.
Here and there the sun pierced through the dense
shade of the trees. It seemed as though all its
rays were setting up ladders of light and were
descending like thieves to steal flowers from the
dark forest. Birds were peeping out from holes
in the tree trunks, their red and black beaks
looking as if the trees had put on red and black
leaves. In some places, on the huge trunks of
some big trees, it seemed as if a whole village of

birds were situated in the branches. In other places rows of tall palms lifted their graceful heads and with their fronds joined together, like the wings of birds, made a cool darkness in the woods. In other places, through breaks in the forest, sparkling chatim trees looked up to the sky holding their leaves aloft like beautiful fingers. Great creepers joined tree to tree like bridges, and in some places seemed to have prepared swings for the spirits of the wood to play in. Utonka saw wild boars, some of them digging up the earth, and some lying in holes. Now and then he saw two huge curved horns appear behind the screen of distant trees, and once or twice a forest deer started suddenly from right before him. Once he saw on the branch of a tree a big honeycomb with black bees buzzing round it.

After some time Utonka entered a large open plain. In the distance the scorching sunlight was flickering like tongues of fire. The sky was deep blue.

Before going out into the heat of the sun Utonka sat down to rest in the shade at the edge of the forest. Suddenly, as if from nowhere, a huge black cow appeared in the middle of the plain. How wonderful! Whence could it have come? Utonka had no idea that there was such a large cow anywhere in the world, and he rubbed his eyes to make sure he was not dreaming. When he had stopped rubbing his eyes he was still more astonished; for on the back of the cow there was now a tall radiant figure. Utonka stood up in his astonishment.

Perhaps you are thinking that Utonka ran away, but if you had been there you would certainly have stood motionless as he did to see that huge cow. From its neck hung fold upon fold of well grown dewlap and on its head were two shining sharp horns of great length. Its legs were covered with soft white hair almost to the ankle and it had a huge tail white in colour and gradually tapering till it almost touched the ground.

It seemed as if light was coming from its broad black forehead. On its back was a strong man with shining bare body. So enchanting was the beauty of this sight, that Utonka stood overwhelmed with wonder and astonishment.

As he stood looking at the cow it seemed as if, in the twinkling of an eye, it came right up to him from the place where it had been standing without apparently moving its limbs. In great astonishment Utonka looked up at it and saw two large black and lustrous eyes gazing at him. On seeing those eyes the whole of Utonka's body felt a pleasant coolness like that which one feels on drinking very cool water. Raising his face a little Utonka saw two bright eyes looking at him from a face wreathed in smiles. As he looked into those eyes he heard, as though in a dream, a voice say to him, "My child, drink some of the milk of this cow; for your Guru also has done so." Utonka then bent down to drink and, as he drank, it tasted to him like nectar.

But when he lifted his head after drinking he discovered that the cow and its rider had disappeared and there was no sign of their having been there at all. The plain was flooded with the blazing sun-light. Near by was the dense forest with its shade and from it the sound of birds and bees could be heard. Squirrels with their pretty striped bodies were running out into the open from the shelter of the woods and they would then peep round and, starting suddenly, run back into the safety of the forest.

Utonka feeling much astonished said to himself, "Was it then all a dream? Have I been asleep? It will never do for me to fall asleep like this and dream on my journey. I have to bring back that offering. I wonder how far I am from the king's palace?"

Thus thinking to himself he set off at a great pace, but all the time he kept saying, "What have I seen? Has some god shown himself to me?" And as he questioned thus he imperceptibly began to slacken his pace.   When, however, he remembered the offering he hastened on again.

CHAPTER V

Utonka arrived at the palace of king Poshya in the evening and thought he would try to get the ear-rings and return the same night. So without any delay he went straight to the king and told him what he wanted. The king, after saluting him with deep respect and giving him water for his tired feet, asked him first to wash his hands and mouth and rest a little. "Why are you in a hurry?" he said. "You can get what you want by going yourself to the inner apartments of the Queen."

Utonka replied, "Oh, king, may you live long and prosper. I wanted to return with the ear-rings this very night, but if that is not possible, let me at least ask for them at once. For so long as I am in doubt I shall have no peace of mind."

The king laughed slightly and said: "Very well. Go into the palace. The doorkeeper will show you the way. I myself am going to my evening worship and cannot come with you." Saying this the king bowed low to Utonka and turned away. Utonka was over-joyed and raising his two hands in blessing turned to follow the doorkeeper into the inner apartments.

In every room of the palace lamps were twinkling in the dusk of evening. On the altar, in the fire temple, was seated the fire god wearing a glowing crown of flame, while chanting was heard to the accompaniment of the evening bells. On entering the inner palace Utonka saw a large Bokul tree in a courtyard round which the darkness was gathering,—on all sides from the windows of the palace the light of lamps was falling and making the leaves seem black and shining in the distance. At the foot of this tree a large cow was standing, its body a beautiful pale red, looking dark in the evening gloom. On her forehead was a white crescent moon and the white dust near her feet looked very beautiful. From the body of the cow came a sweet scent which seemed to fill the air with peace, while in front were seated several girls dressed in red silk and burning incense by the light of lamps.

In one of the rooms the doorkeeper stopped and said: "Brahmachari, wait a little in this room, while I go to call the Queen. She will make her obeisance to you in the next room." Saying which, the doorkeeper went towards the cow, while Utonka sat down and waited.

As he was waiting it seemed to Utonka that there was on all sides a calm and blessed peace pervading the atmosphere. He saw the Queen's attendants moving about in the court-yard from place to place with lamps in their hands and dressed in red silk. By the light of the lamps their faces appeared bright and beautiful, full of joy and peace. At last the door-keeper came and called him. Utonka, following slowly, entered a room in the middle of which a clear bright light was burning. A soft scent came from the sweet smelling oil. On all sides incense was rising—but in the room itself there was nothing; it was absolutely empty.

When he entered, Utonka could see no one, but the doorkeeper pointed to a seat inlaid with mother-of-pearl for him to sit on. As he took his seat he asked the doorkeeper, "Has the queen not come yet?"

The doorkeeper replied with evident astonishment, "Why there she is sitting on that shell-covered seat wearing a red dress. Can't you see her?"

Although Utonka looked hard he could see nothing whatever, and he exclaimed, "What do you say? Are you joking with me? Where is the queen sitting? I can see nothing."

The old doorkeeper laughed and said, "Brahmachari, do not be angry with me; but you must, I suppose, be impure and that is why you cannot see the Queen."

Then the Brahmachari recollected his vision at the edge of the forest and said to himself, "Then that was not really a dream after all. Everything was real and because I have not washed my mouth after drinking that milk, therefore I am impure and cannot see the queen. But I thought the whole thing was a dream. How wonderful the glory of this queen must be."

So Utonka rose quickly and went away to wash. Having washed his hands and mouth the Brahmachari returned and the glory of the Queen was revealed to him. She was seated on a seat which was decorated with exquisite pearls. Her dress was made of red silk. Her face was so radiant that the very gold of her ear-rings appeared dull in comparison, and the beauty of her smile was like a flower or a star. Gazing at her it seemed to Utonka that his brow had been cooled with dewdrops and he was not able to take his eyes off her. He thought that the palace in which such a woman lived must indeed be a habitation fit for the gods.

Meanwhile the Queen had come down from her seat and was making her obeisance to Utonka. Just as blossoms are shaken from the Shal tree by passing breezes, so it seemed as if blessings were showered from Utonka's heart. He said, "May eternal good fortune attend you. Mother, I request one gift from your generous hands. Give me your ear-rings." Queen Shubashukla laughing gently, removed the ear-rings with a graceful gesture, bending her head as she did so. Just then, a companion of the queen entered the room with a tray on which were honey, curds, sandal paste, paddy and a cluster of Bokul leaves.* The Queen taking this tray from her companion's hands placed the two ear-rings on it and laid it at the feet of Utonka making an obeisance as she did so. Utonka accepting the offering lifted up the two ear-rings to look at them. Then the Queen said in a sweet voice, "Brahmachari, take care of them, for the king

---

* These are given as a sign of respect to an honoured guest.

of the snakes has shown a great desire to pos-
sess them."

"Very well," said Utonka as he stood up and
blessed the Queen. "May peace be with you
and waft its unseen breezes to cool your heart."

Full of joy Utonka left the inner apartments
with the doorkeeper, whereupon Shubashukla
embracing her companion said laughing, "To-
day my companion I am very happy; for by
giving these worthless gold ear-rings to this
Brahmachari I have been made holier." At
which her companion laughed and said, "We
also share your happiness, but I hope that
Takshat will not cause any trouble to him on
the road."

Shubashukla replied: "Even if any accident
happens, who would hurt the Brahmachari?
The gods would conspire together to return the
ear-rings to him, if they were lost or stolen."

In the meantime Utonka, taking the ear-rings
with him, wondered, as he went out, at the
beauty and grace of the palace. On his way he

met the king who was returning from his evening prayers carrying some flowers in his hands. Seeing the Brahmachari he greeted him by scattering flowers over him.

Utonka addressing him said: "My prayer, oh king, has been granted.   I have obtained the gift and must now bid farewell."

The king replied: "But I cannot bid farewell so soon.   Stay at least to-night."   So Utonka stayed that night in the palace.

All the noise of birds and beasts and men was stilled and in the depth of the night Utonka began to think about the splendour of the royal palace.   It seemed to him that heavenly messengers were descending through the moonligh and were standing all round the palace singing sacred chants in soft tones.   Then again he remembered with wonder his vision of that cow.   Then his mind turned to thoughts of his Guru's wife and of his fellow students all of whom he was so soon to leave.   All the hundreds of events that had happened to him since his childhood in the ashram came before him and so he kept on thinking till it struck midnight. Then keeping tight hold of the ear-rings, and uttering the name of his Guru, Utonka turned over and went to sleep.

CHAPTER VI

In the fields there is neither man nor beast. Overhead is the intense burning sun. But a strong wind has sprung up and is raising a white dust in the eyes of the sun. Look in the distance and you will see that all the leaves and branches of the forest are dancing like mad elephants striking their trunks against each other's bodies, while all the time a hissing panting sound can be heard. Along the fields storms of dust, like hordes of white frenzied ghosts, are tearing along, sometimes turning round and round and sometimes rising high in gigantic forms.

There seems to be not a cloud in the sky. Only under those trees the sky in the distance is dark and lowering and all the time the mad breeze blows strongly.

Who is this who speeds along with scarf flying in the wind, like the wings of a bird as it struggles for its life with all its might against the storm? Who but our Utonka returning to the ashram with the ear-rings?

Utonka having left the open fields is taking shelter behind a tree. Take care, Utonka, be careful of your precious ear-rings! For this is the very field where that mysterious cow appeared to you and made you drink its milk— all sorts of unearthly things happen here. It seemed as though Utonka realised his danger; for he sat down carefully and said, "I will see whether I can discover the meaning of what happened to me yesterday."

For a long time he looked steadfastly in the direction of the dusty field but he could see nothing. On looking behind him however he saw a curious sight. He saw, at a height of two or three feet from the ground, a tall beggar with shaven head, ugly and almost naked, coming towards him. His face was clean shaven and his cheeks wrinkled, while on his forehead were three or four dreadful black lines, and as he approached he kept making hideous grimaces. Crouching down, he beat his hands all the time against his hollow sides. It almost seemed as if a dust-storm, vexed by the wind was trying to drag this object along in its clutches.

Utonka began to wonder whatever was the matter, but at that very moment the beggar disappeared. Utonka burst out laughing at having been deceived by such a curious image and illusion. But he was again surprised when that half-naked, shaven-headed image appeared floating in the sky, only to disappear again in the twinkling of an eye.

Utonka laughed to himself and thought: "The next time the beggar comes, he will stand right on my head and I shall be able to make Mr. Juggler a captive." Laughing at this thought Utonka stood up suddenly, but the beggar was nowhere to be seen. Instead, Utonka saw the powerful Takshat emerge suddenly like a flash of lightning from a hole five feet away. Darting to Utonka's feet he seized the box containing the ear-rings and leapt back into the hole.

When Utonka realized the clever cunning of the wicked serpent king, he fell into a frenzy of despair. But when he had managed to calm his mind, he began to pray to Indra saying, "Oh, mighty Indra, whose thunderbolt can shatter a rock to atoms and can burn the whole world to ashes, now help this poor helpless Brahmachari. Oh, Indra, whose clouds afford a grateful shade to the hot and weary traveller and give water to the thirsty, and abundant crops to your worshippers, help this poor and helpless Brahmachari."

Looking up to heaven Utonka prayed thus with folded hands, and as he gazed into the sky a cloud descended and floated just above his head. A little later Utonka felt a gentle rain falling and then a rainbow appeared, and from one side of the cloud to the other bright flashes sparkled and danced. Utonka saw some one sitting in the middle of that dark cloud who encouraged him with loving smiles. He gazed steadfastly and, as he gazed, the cloud descended still lower with a gentle patter of rain, and at last, drenching Utonka with its dew, it entered the earth. The ground opened as though struck by a thunder-bolt. Sitting on the rainbow, in the middle of that dark cloud, Utonka descended into the nether regions. As he entered the womb of the earth he saw suspended on all sides of his cloudy chariot the tops of many sweet-scented trees with crowds of bright coloured insects fluttering in their branches. Seated on the cloud he felt a pleasing coolness until suddenly he ceased to move.

CHAPTER VII

The nether regions are merely a pleasing fancy of the poets. For the nourishment of a tree, air and light are needed outside, while inside is needed the cool sap drawn from the dark regions underground. So, also, this vast earth needs sap, as the tree does, to give it strength.

When the minds and imaginations of the poets were filled with the beauty, immensity and power of the world and the stars and planets, then in the joy of that power and energy they tried to express the rhythmic movement of the spirit of the universe and the idea of this inner energy in many varied images.

The nether regions were to them a bottomless storehouse from which the world, standing like

a huge branching tree, draws its nourishment.
Just as the roots of a tree are in the ground,
from which it draws cool sap, so the roots of the
world descend into the lower regions. That
energy which you see expressed in the world in
light and in flashes of lightning has also been
gathered up and stored in the hidden chambers
of the nether regions. And those changing
pictures of the seasons which you see as the
years pass over the world are but the reflection
of original paintings which are there also; while
the ever new days and nights in the world are
but the play of a power hidden there.

In this storehouse many wonderful things are
kept. Therefore these regions are full of terror.
No one dare enter them alone. Fearful serpents
go round and round hissing fiercely,—sentinels
keep guard over great heaps of jewels and pearls.
Over these there always hangs a thick gloomy
haze like a cloud, from which every now
and then in the stillness there darts a sudden
flash of lightning. Here the wind blows keenly

and is not restless like our breezes. It blows silently and constantly with a piercing chill. Deep echoes like thousands of conch shells blown together sound on all sides.

Arriving at the entrance to these regions Utonka heard, as he came to a standstill, a sound like the roar of the mighty sea. He was astounded and you can understand how alert his mind was at that moment. The darkness and that roaring sound filled his mind with fear and doubt, but after remaining for a long time motionless with fear he began to concentrate his mind and sat down to meditate on Indra.

You must remember that if you have the power of deep concentration and can meditate, you can realize God's presence at any time; for He is present at all times and in all places. Utonka was a true Brahmachari so he had acquired considerable power of concentration. While he was plunged in deep meditation a dreadful sound pierced the darkness a little to

Utonka's right, as if the light of a flaming fire
had suddenly been revealed and with a solemn
note a sweet voice sounded in his ear saying,
"Utonka, enter this room."

As Utonka got up he saw a bright and beautiful flaming light and he started with surprise.
Then his mind was filled with intense joy.
Often in the darkness of the night-time he had
risen to adore the blazing fire; and to-day in
the darkness of the nether regions his life had
in a moment become full of power through the
radiance of this great blazing light.

Utonka began to advance towards this light
uttering a chant of adoration as he did so. But
on getting closer to it he found that it was not
a fire at all but a huge golden door that shone
with intense brightness. He thought with a
certain amount of shame, "Alas I have been
worshipping a mere door of gold as if it were
fire. But perhaps I shall find the god of fire
within this room." Then he approached the
door and no sooner had he touched it than it

was blown open by a strong gust of wind. On entering he saw a wonderful sight. A huge room filled with white light in the middle of which, glowing like a blazing fire, stood a horse with large wide open eyes. By its side a strong man was standing, while, surrounding it on all sides were six beautifully dressed boys dancing wildly and every moment throwing off one dress and putting on a new one. Sitting a little distance away were two exquisitely beautiful damsels on golden thrones busily weaving cloth upon a loom with threads of two colours, one bright like the golden colour of their bodies, the other jet black like their hair. They were every moment throwing the cloth on to the bodies of the boys who, laughing merrily, kept picking up this cloth and putting it on. On one side two guards were standing motionless.

Utonka became more and more astonished as he looked upon this scene. These two guards seemed so strong that it looked as if they could easily overpower that radiant horse of fire.

Their bodies were so upright and full of energy
and their arms were so straight that it seemed
as if they could at any moment overcome the
most powerful lion and yet from the look on
their faces they appeared to be tranquil and
smiling angels.

Utonka now turned to look at the man who
was standing beside the horse. On examining
him closely he recognised him as the same man·
who had shown himself seated on the cow which
had appeared to him on the plain. Then the
man said with a gentle smile, "My child take
this horse outside, breathe once in his nostrils
and you will get back the ear-rings." Utonka
stupified with wonder took the horse out and in
accordance with the man's command he blew
strongly in the horse's nostrils. As he did so
the hair of the horse's body stood on end and
gradually from every hair fire came out. Without any sound the fire consumed the whole of
the nether regions in a moment of time so that

there was not a trace of them left. But curiously enough the fire did not touch Utonka's body at all. He called out in a loud voice "Now my worship of the fire has borne some fruit. Oh, powerful Fire, I salute thee. Oh, beautiful Fire, I salute thee. Oh, mighty Fire, take me in a golden chariot to the foundations of the earth. Oh, god of Fire, now I understand that it is your throne that is spread in these mysterious lower regions and to thee, oh glorious one, I bow."

After this joyful salutation Utonka looked in front of him, his face bright with the rays of the brilliant fire which spread on all sides, quivering and scarlet like the blossoms of a Dhah tree. There in front of him he saw Takshat who, driven mad by the dreadful heat of the flames, was in full retreat, having thrown down in his haste those ear-rings which lay like golden flowers at Utonka's feet. As soon as he had disappeared the fire gathered itself together and entered the horse's body again.

Utonka having picked up the ear-rings was about to say something when he suddenly realised that the whole vision had vanished. He saw on all sides of him the fresh sunshine of dawning day falling through the trees, the dew on the leaves was not yet dry, the birds were singing, while in front of him was flowing the very stream which passed the ashram of his Guru.

For some time Utonka remained motionless with wonder and astonishment, but at last he stood up laughing and exclaimed "Ugh! I have been dreaming again." Then meditatively and with eyes half closed he went slowly towards the ashram.

As he approached he saw that many Brahmin guests were seated in a circle, their faces radiant with joy, while his Guru Ved was in the centre. They all looked with veneration to the place where the Guru's wife was seated. She was expressing some anxiety because of Utonka's delay, "Everyone has come," she was saying;

"but why is Utonka so late? Can some accident have happened to him on the way?" To this Ved replied at once, "Do not be anxious for he will be here immediately." Even as he spoke Utonka appeared from behind a screen of jasmine flowers and at the same moment the eyes of both the Guru and his wife met his own.

All were delighted as Utonka first of all did obeisance to his Guru and his Guru's wife laying the precious ear-rings at their feet. Then he saluted the rest of the company. The woman's eyes filled with tears of joy as she took the ear-rings, then she went towards the house looking at them as she went.

After receiving the Guru's blessing Utonka stood quietly at one side of the assembly. Then he began to speak, saying, "Gurudev, to-day I have tasted of the limitless energy of the world. My discipline has borne fruit. Plunging into the nether regions I have seen the beauty of day and night, the restless dancing of the six seasons, and all the imperishable forms of beauty in this world. The god of Fire has set his seal upon me and the glory of the hidden fire has filled my mind with wonder. Indra has taken up his abode on the throne of my heart. My life in the world will now be successful. Gurudev, I pray that your blessing may be a constant benediction and help to me."

Having said this Utonka came and sat at his Guru's feet and asked for permission to depart. His Guru Ved gave an affectionate farewell blessing, saying, "My son, may your mind always be happy, and may your work in the world be fruitful. May nobility of purpose, like a flower, blossom in your heart. May all my pupils be able, like you, to accomplish their noble purposes."

CONCLUSION

At last our story is finished. Need we say any more about that constant nobility of purpose which blossomed in the heart of our Utonka?

My prayer is that you also may learn to appreciate the deeper mysteries of this universe, that you may be able to admire the beauty of a pure and noble life and treasure at all times the blessing of your teachers.

May their blessing, uniting with the clouds, fall upon you like gentle rain. Mingling with the sunlight every day at dawn may it manifest itself to your eyes. Breathing in the wind may it bring deep peace into your hearts.   May your minds be happy and filled with the joy and energy of the universe.   May your lives in the world be fruitful,—may nobility of purpose ever blossom in your hearts.   May you also be strong, fearless and pure; and may you accomplish your spiritual destiny by devoting yourselves to God.

Om, Shanti, Shanti, Shanti.   Om, Peace, Peace, Peace.

Printed in the United Kingdom
by Lightning Source UK Ltd.
132369UK00002B/216/A

9 781417 909568